This book is dedicated to all who cherish

America's history as a vast heritage of people and events—some

heroic, some inglorious, but all part of America's epic struggle

to come of age—and to all who know that understanding

the past is essential to dealing with the present.

STATUE OF LIBERTY
THE STORY BEHIND THE SCENERY®

by Paul Weinbaum

Paul Weinbaum, career professional with the National Park Service, is active in preserving and interpreting our cultural and historic resources. He received his doctorate in history from the University of Rochester. As the former curator of the Statue of Liberty National Monument, Paul is extremely knowledgeable about the statue and has a sensitive appreciation for the special significance that this great symbol has for people the world over.

Front and inside covers: Statue of Liberty, Liberty Island. Photos by K. C. DenDooven. Title page: Sunset silhouette. Photo by William Albert Allard/Image Bank. Pages 2–3: "Mother of Exiles." Photo by Margo Conte/Earth Scenes; poem by Emma Lazarus.

Book design by K. C. DenDooven

Third Printing, 1988 • Revised Edition
STATUE OF LIBERTY: THE STORY BEHIND THE SCENERY. © 1988 KC PUBLICATIONS, INC.
LC 88-080652. ISBN 0-88714-023-8

Give me your tired, your poor,
Your huddled masses yearning to breathe free,
The wretched refuse of your teeming shore.
Send these, the homeless, tempest-tost to me,
I lift my lamp beside the golden door!

The Statue of Liberty, that uniquely American symbol that stands in lonely grandeur within New York harbor, has now observed her hundredth birthday. Since her dedication in 1886 she has seen the New York skyline, which once she dwarfed, take on a totally new character, its silhouetted canyons of steel and stone visible for miles. She has seen world wars fought and won, new philosophies of brotherhood emerge, and a self-isolating, individualistic nation change into a democratic world power abounding border to border in productivity, technology, prosperity, and wealth, the likes of which the world has never seen before.

Liberty Enlightening the World, the generous gift of the French people that stands on American soil, began life as an ambassadress of friendship, expressing eloquently the affinity between *Liberté, Égalité, Fraternité* and "Life, Liberty, and the Pursuit of Happiness."

Her baptismal name seems somewhat quaint to us now, for nineteenth-century society was given to bestowing grand titles on its works of art, but it *was* prophetic. The colossal statue conceived more than a century ago by a French sculptor of mixed extraction, has become known throughout the world as a symbol that is unique to America. Her welcoming form has eagerly been sought by millions of people who have come to these shores in search of a better life and political and religious freedom. Embodying the best within us, she is a stoic, enduring, beloved figure whose strong, steady gaze and outstretched arm seem to offer compassion, security, hope, guidance, and—above all—freedom.

The America that the French so idealized a century ago is still here. That our belief in the individual, in the face of political and economic privilege, no longer seem unusual reflects its widespread acceptance. Lest we be tempted to disparage the ideals of our forefathers as simplistic and old-fashioned, let us remember that these ideals have made us one people and motivate us still.

Let Liberty, then, remain the symbolic, vigilant guardian of American ideals and the physical reminder of our origins. And let us ensure that the promise she offers in her upraised light is a true and an enduring one.

America received its independence in the eighteenth century, and for nearly a hundred years republicanism, as a form of government, continued to divide the Americas from monarchical Europe. France was an exception among the European nations (as were Switzerland, Andorra, and San Marino); it had experienced two short-lived republics—the first in the 1790s following the French Revolution and the second between 1848 and 1852. But longer-lived monarchies and em-

The Colossal Vision

pires replaced them; the majority of the French people swore loyalty to the idea of kingship. The political framework began to change only in 1870, when French losses in the Franco-Prussian War led to the downfall of Napoleon III's empire and to the establishment of France's Third Republic.

But long before this, among the French intellegentsia, there was resistance to monarchy as a form of government. The ideas and emotions that had flamed into the French Revolution many decades before had never been extinguished, and to many Frenchmen, America's republican government was the embodiment of a French ideal, a working example of *Liberté, Égalité, Fraternité* in an age of reason.

It is to one of these Frenchman that we owe the idea behind the creation of *La Liberté Éclairant le Monde* ("Liberty Enlightening the World," shortened familiarly to *Liberty*, and now known as the *Statue of Liberty*). A colossal monument

Liberty's colossal torch is her single most powerful symbol. Reconstructed for the 1986 restoration in the original manner that Bartholdi designed, its solid gold covering assures maximum reflection of light and avoidance of future tarnishing.

The torch-bearing arm is 42 feet long; the hand is 16 feet; the index finger is 8 feet. Liberty herself is even larger than she seems when viewed with the island and the harbor as the nearest reference points. Her head is 10 feet from ear to ear; her nose is 4 feet, 6 inches; her mouth is 3 feet; and her eye is 2 feet, 6 inches. She weighs a stupendous 450,000 pounds (225 tons), exclusive of pedestal.

built in an age of monument building, it has fulfilled the prophetic mission proclaimed in its title and even expanded it to become the most revered symbol of America, an image that eclipses even the flag in the emotional response she kindles in the hearts of millions. "She is everywhere even when unseen."

Edouard de Laboulaye—distinguished jurist, professor, popular lecturer—was an ardent ad-mirer of America's republicanism and an expert on American constitutional history. It was he who in 1865 hosted the now legendary dinner in which the idea of Liberty was conceived, and it is he who is generally considered its father. Also present was Frédéric Auguste Bartholdi, who, although then only thirty-one, cut quite a figure in the realm of popular sculpture. (It is to his published account that we owe the story. The

quoted words are Bartholdi's own.)

In the fervent atmosphere of the dinner conversation, the matter of international gratitude arose, and Laboulaye, quick to embark upon a favorite subject, described the relationship between France and the United States as characterized not so much by gratitude for the Frenchmen who fought and spilled their blood in the American Revolution, as by a "genuine flow of sympathy" in fighting side by side for the "principles that they hoped to see prevail in [America], France, and in the world." The American public, Laboulaye believed, "love Lafayette and his volunteers as they revere the American heroes." This feeling of shared commitment, he said, was an "indestructible basis" of friendship, unlike such political actions as the Treaty of Versailles, "which made the United States what they are" and is now almost forgotten. And further, "If a monument were to be built in America as a memorial to their independence, I should think it very natural if it were built by united efforts, if it were a common work of both nations."

Years later, when this vision had become reality and Bartholdi's Liberty was awaiting the completion of her pedestal, the sculptor recollected that "The conversation interested me so deeply that it remained fixed in my memory." So deeply, apparently, that when Laboulaye later reasserted his views and urged Bartholdi to go to America to see if he could "find a happy idea, a plan that will excite public enthusiasm," the sculptor enthusiastically agreed. "It was, then, in the convictions of M. Laboulaye," Bartholdi said, that the idea of the Statue of Liberty was born, an idea that would not reach full maturity, however, until twenty-one years after that fateful dinner—and three years after Laboulaye's death.

Egyptian Influences

If to Laboulaye we owe the idea of the monument, it is largely to the influence of ancient Egypt that we owe its colossal size.

Bartholdi first traveled to the land of the pharaohs in 1856, when at the beginning of a career that was already off to a good start. He shared the general fascination with Egypt that had been kindled back in 1799 with the discovery of the Rosetta Stone, which made it possible to decipher the enigma of ancient Egyptian hieroglyphics. The great antiquity of the pyramids affected the idealistic Bartholdi, and their colossal size appears to have intensified in him his own preference for sculpture on a colossal scale. (As Bartholdi described it in 1885, in modeling Liberty he emulated the bold lines and ample setting that made the pyramids so successful as colossal works of art. He also commented on other Egyptian colossi, reflecting that "their kindly and impassable glance seems to ignore the present and to be fixed upon an unlimited future.")

Bartholdi traveled again to Egypt in 1869, to attend the opening of the Suez Canal, built under French direction and with French capital. (Subsequently the French also rebuilt much of Egypt's two leading cities, Alexandria and Cairo.) This effort elevated Egypt's ruling Ismail Pasha to the status of "modernizer" of his country. Many international figures were at hand, eager to offer their services for such an ambitious undertaking. Bartholdi was one such individual, and it was in pursuit of a special commission that he had come to the canal ceremonies.

Bartholdi had first approached the pasha two years earlier, when the latter visited Paris, and had proposed to the receptive ruler the building of a colossal statue—the figure of a woman, a *fellah* (Egyptian peasant or laborer), holding a torch aloft. "Progress," or "Egypt carrying the light to Asia," would be its theme. The statue would embody the pasha's efforts at modernization and would also serve the new canal as a lighthouse.

Bartholdi worked on the project intermittently over the next two years, and by the time of the 1869 ceremonies he was ready with a final drawing and a small model of the proposed monument. But the ruler had in the meantime grown cool to the plan, and the sculptor lost his grand-scale gamble in Egypt. Bartholdi was not one to retire in defeat, however, and by the end of the year, it was America—not Egypt—that was absorbing all of his attention. The enthusiasm for the American project instilled in him by Laboulaye was becoming a full-grown passion.

The Egyptian project is important in the history of Liberty because of the obvious similarity between the statue and the one proposed for Egypt, a similarity hotly defended by the sculptor. When the charge was made, after Liberty's completion, that the figures (both female and both intended for use on great waterways as lighthouses) held their lights aloft, he countered: "Would they have me make the figure (whatever it might be) hiding the light under its petticoat not to say under a bushel?" The series of study models Bartholdi executed for the Statue of Liberty can indeed be interpreted as showing the figure clearly evolving from the Egyptian fellah into the familiar figure now in New York Harbor. It must be borne in mind, however, that the device of a female figure holding *something* aloft was often used in the art world of Bartholdi's time.

Just why Bartholdi felt so defensive is puzzling. Considering the years the sculptor spent on the Egyptian project, his proposal for an American monument in the same form—a colossal female figure—was quite simply a natural redirection of his work. Perhaps his ire was an extension of his all-too-human indignation at having had, in his own words, "an evilly disposed newspaper say, and others repeat, that I had executed a colossal statue for Egypt, which had not been used, and that I had resold it to the Society of the French-American Union in order that from it might be made the Statue of Liberty." The rankling of such

Several of the statue's symbolic features can best be seen from above. Here Liberty clasps her huge tablet (23 feet, 7 inches long and 13 feet, 7 inches wide), which bears the date of the Declaration of Independence. In keeping with the sculptor's conception of Liberty as a classical goddess, the date is in Roman numerals.

Bartholdi did this sketch, circa 1875, envisioning Liberty in New York Harbor, a site he chose on his first visit to America. He later recalled his first impressions of the harbor: "In the course of the voyage I formed some conceptions of a plan of a monument, but I can say that at the view of the harbor of New York the definite plan was first clear to my eyes. The picture that is presented to the view when one arrives at New York is marvelous; when, after some days of voyaging, in the pearly radiance of a beautiful morning is revealed the magnificent spectacle of those immense cities [New York and Brooklyn], of those rivers extending as far as the eye can reach, festooned with masts and flags.... It is thrilling. It is, indeed, the New World, which appears in its majestic expanse, with the ardor of its glowing life."

an unjust accusation in the breast of the sensitive sculptor is then quite understandable, given the many years and considerable energies that were consumed in the conceptual development and the construction of his Liberty.

Bartholdi in America

Bartholdi first referred to the statue as an American project in 1869. His "happy idea" was that the statue would be the French people's gift to the United States on the occasion of the American centennial. In 1871, to explore this possibility, the sculptor traveled to the United States.

The sight of New York Harbor, Bartholdi later said, had an instant effect upon him. Then and there he decided that this—the entrance to the New World, the port through which most of America's commerce passed—was the ideal place for Liberty to stand.

Fired by a new, almost religious zeal, the sculptor's imagination soared. Liberty would take the form of a classical goddess (unlike the Egyptian peasant). Its flaming torch and brilliant crown would together symbolize liberation, dignity, and authority. The seven spikes in the crown would represent liberty radiating to each of the seven continents and seven seas, and at the figure's feet, broken shackles would signify freedom from tyranny. Liberty's distinctive link with the American republic would lie in the tablet that would bear the date of the Declaration of Independence: July 4, 1776. Forgotten now were the old schemes, replaced completely and forever by the new dream, the luster of which would one day shine throughout the entire world.

Bartholdi's visit came at a propitious moment in Franco-American relations; only months before, Napoleon III's Second Empire had been replaced by a French republic, and there was a feeling between the two nations of solidarity and kinship. The sculptor, taking advantage of the heightened climate of good will, established contacts that would prove important to his undertaking. Among these people were John W. Forney, publisher of the Philadelphia *Press* (later to become the representative for America's centennial

Liberty is not as passive as she may seem to some. The just-broken shackles at her feet, for instance, reveal her to be a strong participant in the fight against tyranny.

K. C. DENDOOVEN

MUSEUM OF THE CITY OF NEW YORK

In 1870 Bartholdi completed this terracotta model— 20 inches (52 centimeters) in height. It is one of the few such models to be found in the United States.

exhibition in France) and, through Forney, President Ulysses S. Grant. He also met artist John LaFarge, poet Henry Wadsworth Longfellow, and architect H. H. Richardson—all leading figures within their respective disciplines—and was introduced to the New York French community, which would later prove such a boon in the support of his monument.

On this, the first of four trips Bartholdi made to America, he traveled the length and breadth of the country, all the while steadfastly promoting his project. Awed by the physical grandeur of the American West and impressed with the country's technological accomplishments, his enthusiasm was boundless; and, while he perhaps thought most Americans disconcertingly direct and hurried, he liked them heartily and admired tremendously their ability to build cities and develop land at a breathtaking pace. Europe had limiting conceptions of time and scale—limits that he saw did not apply to America. The sculptor's envisioned colossal statue (referred to as "my American") and its daringness was thus totally in keeping with the American character.

By 1871, then, Bartholdi had completed his initial study models, traveled to the United States,

and even selected the location for his proposed statue. But further work on the project, which he still hoped would be done in time to commemorate America's centennial, would have to wait. The political situation in France was unsettled. France had lost the Franco-Prussian War of 1870 and had to pay Germany an indemnity of five billion francs (about a billion dollars), and until 1873, when that indemnity was paid, German troops occupied eastern France. The republic had been proclaimed in September, 1870, but monarchists continued to dominate the provisional National Assembly which governed France. Meanwhile, Liberty's French supporters declared their intention of commemorating the American republic's centennial only at such time as they had secured a republic on their own soil.

THE UNION FRANCO-AMÉRICAINE

When the Assembly approved a republican constitution in December, 1875, the Liberty project (announced publicly in 1874) was off to a good start. The month before, on November 6, 1875, a great banquet, attended by influential Frenchmen of many political persuasions, was held in official recognition of the organization of the Union

Liberty's head and upper torso were completed for display at the Paris Universal Exhibition of 1878. Visitors who wished to see the interior were charged admission; the money raised in this way helped pay for the costs of the construction work then underway. The plaque identifies the exhibit as the "Monument de L'Independance, La Liberté Éclairant le Monde."

Franco-Américaine. Edouard de Laboulaye, Bartholdi's long-time collaborator, was the union's first president, and it included some of France's most famous citizens, including descendants of American Revolutionary heroes Lafayette and Rochambeau. The plan was that the project would be a joint effort of the two nations—the statue to be completed and transported to the United States by the French people, and the pedestal upon which the statue would stand to be designed, built, and paid for by the Americans.

The drive for French funds met with a warm and instantaneous response, and Bartholdi was at long last able to begin actual construction of Liberty. Money came from 181 municipalities and over a hundred thousand individuals. Many special benefits and events were held, some better received than others. The famous composer Gounod wrote a special "Liberty Cantata" which was presented by the Paris Opera. Authorized models of the statue brought in some proceeds, as did the sale of one-franc (twenty-cent) lottery tickets for a department-store drawing for 528 prizes (including a $4,000 table service) and admission tickets to the interior of the head of the statue, which was displayed at the Paris Universal Exhibition in 1878. Efforts to keep the statue in the public eye were constant, and by 1881 the Union Franco-Américaine had raised the equivalent of the statue's cost of $400,000—the cost having swollen from the estimate of $250,000 because of the difficulties encountered in construction and the experimental nature of the work.

THE AMERICAN COMMITTEE

On the other side of the Atlantic, matters weren't going as well, and it was not until January, 1877, that the American division of the Union Franco-Américaine was formed, called simply the "American Committee" and at first comprising a membership of about a hundred (increased to four hundred over the committee's ten-year existence). It included such prominent citizens as industrialist Samuel D. Babcock, social reformer John Jay, poet and newspaper editor William Cullen Bryant, railroad executive and first president of the Metropolitan Museum of Art John Taylor Johnson, former Ohio governor and U.S. Minister to France Edwin F. Noyes. The committee was headed by noted jurist William M. Evarts, soon to become U.S. Secretary of State. J. W. Pinchot was treasurer, and Richard Butler served as secretary and contact with the sculptor. Politicians, business-men, philanthropists, art connoisseurs, Americans of French descent (New Yorkers mostly)—these were the people who comprised the American Committee, whose major responsibility was to raise the $125,000 it estimated was needed to build Liberty's pedestal.

At the time the committee was formed, Bartholdi had just paid an eight-month visit to the United States to oversee the display of Liberty's right arm and torch (on whose platform visitors delighted in standing), at America's centennial exhibition in Philadelphia, for which Liberty had originally been intended. The French gift had been officially acknowledged, and in February, 1877, Congress authorized the setting aside of a site for the statue and—once the statue and pedestal had been erected with private funds—the provision of funds for its permanent maintenance.

The problem lay in collecting the *private* funds. The American Committee, despite the great diversity of its membership, was a project of the wealthy. Of the $161,000 raised by November, 1884, only $7,000 was donated in amounts of less than $100, more than the average citizen at that time made in a month. Gifts of hundreds or thousands of dollars came in from businesses and prominent individuals such as John Jacob Astor, Cyrus W. Field (famed for the first transatlantic cable), steel magnate Andrew Carnegie, and showman P. T. Barnum. In addition, the New York Art Loan Exhibition brought in nearly $14,000 from admissions for viewing works of art and decorative objects loaned by supporters.

Contributions had grown to $180,000 by 1885, but the pedestal's original estimated cost had now doubled, and several times lack of money had halted construction, begun the year before.

Relevant to the financial difficulties faced by the committee was the fact that the idea of Bartholdi's colossal statue—while warmly received by the French, accustomed as they were to grand statements of art—was given a rather lukewarm reception by the Americans, who had few such precedents. In fact, many were downright skeptical, amused, or even hostile to the whole idea. "Pagan goddess," was typical of the unflattering epithets appearing in the press. To the pragmatic American viewing the huge torch on exhibit, even the sculptor's sanity was suspect. Moreover, it seemed to be, aside from a project of the rich, New York's particular responsibility.

Finally, in March of 1885, with the statue itself completed and awaiting shipment in France, the American Committee issued an impassioned

Liberty's right forearm and torch were displayed in 1876 at America's centennial exhibition in Philadelphia. Visitors delighted in being photographed on its balcony. The sheen of the then-new, penny-colored copper is apparent in this old photo.

"Appeal to Patriotism," its first public solicitation:

> *If the money is not now forthcoming the statue must return to its donors, to the everlasting disgrace of the American people, or it must go to some other city, to the everlasting dishonor of New York. Citizens of the State, citizens of the metropolis, we ask you . . . to prevent so painful and humiliating a catastrophe: We ask you, one and all, each according to his means, to contribute what he is able. . . . [and] not to neglect this last opportunity for securing to yourselves and to the Nation an imperishable glory.*

Thousands of small donations did indeed save the day, but that occurred largely through the timely and energetic interest taken by Joseph Pulitzer, publisher of the New York *World*.

The *World's* Campaign

Pulitzer's fund-raising campaign began in earnest on March 16, 1885, just one week before

UNCLE SAM'S AWKWARDNESS.

New Arrival from France—"*Ah, Monsieur Oncle Sam! Escort me to my pedestal, s'il vous plait.*"

Uncle Sam—"*H'm. Well, you see, the fact is, Miss Liberty, we've only had ten years' notice to get the tarnation thing ready, so it isn't quite finished yet. But I reckon it will be complete by the time you get through the Barge Office.*"

the American Committee issued its own appeal. The *World*, in a front-page editorial, blasted the rich for not having come up with the "pittance" necessary to accept Liberty and appealed to American pride, lifting the project from a local to a national issue by forcefully pointing out that the statue was a gift to *all* the American people, paid for by the masses of the French people. "Let us respond in like manner. Let us not wait for the millionaires to give the money." Furthermore, the "people's paper" promised, it would publish the names of every giver, no matter how small the amount. The April 22 issue rhapsodized:

> What a magnificent object it will be as it towers out of the beautiful harbor up almost into the clouds! It will be the first thing to which every newcomer to these shores will look. It will stand as a mountain-like symbol of Liberty before the eyes of every man who comes hence from the oppressed countries beyond the ocean. . . . it signalizes the fullest achievement of human freedom, and it will stand forever to tell that story.

Liberty's cause was a natural for Joseph Pulitzer. His own life had been greatly influenced by American ideals of liberty. He had emigrated from Hungary in the midst of the Civil War. After serving in the Union Army, he attained prominence in the local politics of St. Louis as publisher of the *Post Dispatch*. In 1883 he bought the *World*, moved to New York, and began searching for a way to

establish his paper's reputation. Liberty *was* a good cause and, as it turned out, a successful one. The pedestal fund-raising campaign made the *World's* circulation the largest in the western hemisphere and brought Pulitzer, self-styled "people's journalist," fame.

Gone now was the animosity toward "New York's lighthouse." The contributions came pouring in, often more than a thousand per day and, true to its word, the *World* printed names—long lists of them—and amounts given. Contributions of 10¢, 25¢, and 50¢ were ordinary. By April, a month into the campaign, it "assumed the same popular character that distinguished and glorified it in Paris." Shop-girls, workingmen, civil servants, people from all walks of life from New York (and throughout the country) donated. As in France, special benefits—theatrical performances, sporting events, and balls—were held to bring in money for Liberty, taken into the large heart of America and now a cause célèbre throughout the land.

And day after day the editorializing continued: "Gather in the money dollar by dollar, dime by dime, penny by penny."

The stories of the school children's donations made good copy. "See what the children are doing," the *World* agitated. A nine-year-old boy collected $7 from his father's employees; a thirteen-year-old girl raised funds from among a hundred of her schoolmates; a grammar-school girl "made her papa, her brother and all the family subscribe, as well as all the people who came into her papa's store."

Any item that might keep the issue before the public was published. Stories of gifts of pet chickens and a gold-headed cane added interest to the campaign; cartoons, poems, and editorials criticizing rival newspapers added literary fervor to the general excitement. New impetus was given to the drive when word came from France that the statue was being packed for shipment, and again when her transport, the *Isère*, docked with the precious load in New York Harbor. By August 11, the *World* triumphantly announced that it had achieved the desired $100,000, having received contributions from more than 120,000 people. The popularity of the Liberty project with the citizenry on both sides of the Atlantic had made the fundraising for both Liberty and her pedestal a success—and the culmination of a colossal vision a certainty.

Art and Engineering

At the time the Union Franco-Américaine was formed in 1875, Bartholdi had already made progress on Liberty, in the form of several small study models. Many problems had to be faced concerning the statue's design and construction, problems for which the sculptor had to rely heavily on his own genius, having few precedents to follow. An impressive monument even today, a century ago it was a truly astonishing project. Its 302-foot height (including pedestal) would dominate the late-nineteenth-century skylines of both New York and New Jersey, and its torch would overreach every man-made structure within view.

Liberty would also eclipse any statue that had ever been built up to that time, her extraordinary proportions exceeding the *Colossus of Rhodes*, one of the "Seven Wonders of the Ancient World," and Italy's seventeenth-century *S. Carlo* (St. Charles) *Borromeo*, at a hundred feet the nearest existing statue to the proposed Liberty in height. Thus Liberty, when constructed, would be an engineering tour de force as well as a work of art.

As an artist, Bartholdi was of course the product of his times, and he was heavily influenced by conceptions of *liberty* that had gone before. Notable among the lessons of the past were Delacroix's 1830 *La Liberté Guidant le Peuple*, a symbolic painting of that year's July Revolution so powerful and dynamic in its appeal that it had been branded subversive by the government and consigned to obscurity until a more tolerant political climate allowed its restoration to public view.

Plaster is being applied to the wooden lath of the final, full-scale model of Liberty. Wooden molds were then constructed and shaped around the model. Copper sheeting used for the statue itself was hammered into these molds, in the repoussé method.

The classical features of Liberty radiate an exalted beauty as well as strength.

Bartholdi's Liberty, probably influenced also by the pacifistic Laboulaye, was a much more subdued figure, fully clothed, carrying not a flag and rifle but the passive symbols of tablet and torch. She is a classic goddess radiating in the nimbus of her crown and face the beatitude of a saint, one whose strength is evident in the broken shackles at her feet and whose mission of truth is revealed in the enlightening torch and the Moses-like tablet in her strong arms.

Her stoic, solemn features are uniquely her own, but to some they reflect, as Bartholdi is said to have admitted, the face of his beloved mother, a widow and herself something of a political vic-tim—a Frenchwoman living in German-controlled Alsace.

The enlargement of Liberty to full scale has been described in some detail by Bartholdi, its creator; by J. B. Gauthier of the firm of Gaget, Gauthier et Cie., in whose workshop Liberty was built; and by Charles Talansier, who presented the engineering data to the French public in the technical journal, *Le Génie Civil.* The accounts refer to the challenge of the task, to the "immense workshop, specially constructed for the work," to the "unusual precision" of the final enlargement, and to the "consummate ability" of the persons involved in the creative process. The statue's con-

Amidst the surprising disarray of the cavernous workshop (above) are the full-scale models of the hand and tablet, the preceding model, and a quarter-sized head. The wooden molds and copper sheets (right) were used for Liberty's final form. The forty workers posing for the photo above are engaged in different phases of the construction, which were carried on simultaneously. These photos are remarkable for their time, given the primitive knowledge of indoor photography then available. They— together with the photos on pages 14 and 18—are the work of Pierre Petit and were originally published in 1883 as part of a limited-edition photographic album that documented the work in progress. The albums were autographed by Bartholdi before being presented to various important personages.

struction and its complexities, together with the public's fascination with size, is without doubt an important part of its story.

The material of which the statue was to be made was a very critical factor. "It must be light, easily worked, of good appearance and yet strong enough to stand the stress of a long ocean voyage—and must be almost impervious to the effect of the salt-laden air of New York Harbor." It was decided to use pure copper, a material which fulfilled all of these requirements. Moreover, it was not as expensive as copper alloy nor as heavy as bronze. The framework would be of iron and steel.

Liberty was executed in the repoussé method: the metal of the outer surface raised in relief by hammering on the reverse side. Repoussé allowed for the use of copper sheets far thinner (2.5 millimeters, or about 3/32 of an inch thick) than casting from a mold would have permitted. Indeed, had the statue been cast (the usual method for producing metal sculpture), the amount of metal required would have been prohibitive in cost and, considering that Liberty was

to be transported across the Atlantic, in terms of weight.

Casting had replaced the repoussé method for creating sculpture in antiquity because it allowed for greater precision of detail, but ironically in creating colossal sculpture—which because of its nature required a great degree of technological sophistication—the more "primitive" method had the advantage. Bartholdi contended that fine detail of the kind that casting permitted would, when used in colossal sculpture, "detract from the general appearance of the work."

The legendary *Colossus of Rhodes* (also a kind of lighthouse) was said to have been executed in the repoussé method. A more conscious precedent for Liberty, however, was the *S. Carlo Borromeo* statue. Bartholdi disparaged this work as not colossal art but as "an ordinary statue enlarged"; he admired it, however, as "the first example of the use of repoussé copper mounted on iron trusses." The 1865 statue of Vercingétorix (Gallic chieftain defeated by Caesar) was also especially influential because, although only about twenty-three feet high, it was done in copper repoussé upon the

recommendation of architect Eugène Emmanuel Viollet-le-Duc, Liberty's first structural engineer, who had been called in early on to deal with the special difficulties that the monumental Liberty presented.

The Process of Enlargement

Liberty reached her ultimate 151-foot height through enlarging a series of models. The first clay figure, 1.25 meters (4$^+$ feet), was enlarged three times in plaster. The first enlargement was made to a height of 2.85 meters (9$^+$ feet), including torch. This model (1/16 scale), was enlarged four-fold to over 11 meters (36$^+$ feet), by what Bartholdi could term the "ordinary processes," since in that day larger-than-life sculpture was very popular. It was at this stage that the sculptor made his last revisions, correcting and refining the model down to the last detail. The third and final enlargement was again fourfold and was done as a set of full-scale segments; the total height of the parts equaled about 46 meters (151 feet).

Essentially, a number of points were used to determine the proportions of lines and surfaces (which would of course remain the same no matter what the model's size), and in full scale these points were connected with strips of wood, forming skeletal-like laths then covered with plaster. Each point required the taking of six measurements—three on the model and three on the enlargement. Verifying measurements had also to be taken. With 300 major points and more than 1,200 secondary points, a total of 9,000 measurements were required for each section.

When the full set of full-scale plaster segments was finished, the shape had to be transferred to the thin copper sheets which would form the fragile skin of the statue, sheets that had been pre-cut into pieces that conformed to the general outlines of the statue. Huge, rigid, lattice-like wooden molds were constructed for this purpose, and the copper sheets were carefully pressed, hand-hammered, and molded to conform to the inner shape of the molds, something like the way the lining of a cap, for instance, takes on the shape of the cap itself. When complex forms were involved, the copper was heated in a forge and lowered into place in the upturned molds. After the

Like a giant jigsaw puzzle, the finished pieces of copper were fitted together. Her armature in place outside the workshop, the incomplete Liberty already towers over nearby buildings. In the foreground her torch and head are incongruously juxtaposed.

Liberty's crown rests upon a modest coiffure reminiscent of the styles of the late nineteenth century. The repetitious lines of the hair suggest the undulating waves of the sea and are an example of the remarkable detail that was attained in the sculpturing of the statue.

sheets were removed from the wooden molds, the copper was hammered on the outer side to develop the detail that hammering on the inner side could not achieve. In the last stage, the completed copper pieces, over 300 in all, were taken out of doors for temporary assembly, as a preview of how Liberty would appear when finally placed in her American home.

THE ARMATURE

The framework that supported the statue was no less inventive. It was designed and executed by Gustave Eiffel, who later built the Eiffel Tower for the French Revolution's centennial in 1889. Like Bartholdi an admirer of the colossal, he came to the Liberty project in 1879 upon the death of Viollet-le-Duc. As France's most renowned builder of railway bridges, Eiffel used his knowledge of iron construction and the mathematics of stress

that he and others, in bridge building, had already proven empirically correct. The high, airy bridges for which he was famous did not rely upon the sheer bulk and weight of masonry for strength. (Oddly, traditionalist Viollet-le-Duc's theoretical solution for the stabilization of Liberty was to fill her interior to the hips with sand!)

In Liberty, Eiffel produced one of the first great curtain-wall construction structures, foreshadowing the late 1880's development of the skyscraper. (Viollet-le-Duc, who had engineered the head of Liberty, already on display, had once suggested that "a practical architect might not unnaturally conceive the idea of erecting a vast edifice whose frame should be entirely of iron. . . .")

Basically, the structure is this: A central pylon 29.54 meters (96 feet, 11 inches), formed by four huge iron posts running from the statue's base, supports the weight of the entire structure. From this central tower extends a network of smaller beams, secondary iron work that conforms to the shape of the figure and tertiary iron bars that connect directly to the iron braces that back and reinforce the shape of the individual copper pieces.

The genius of Eiffel is readily apparent in that each section is supported independently, resting not on the copper plate below it nor hanging from the one above. The skin "floats" with the flexing of the hundreds of parts that make up the suspension system. Thus the whole structure is a single, intricately trussed unit whose elasticity allows it to adjust by subtle degrees to expansion and contraction, making it resistant to the winds that buffet it unevenly on its surfaces.

Rising 12.38 meters (40 feet, 7 inches) above the pylon, a more complex girder forms the center of the arm, narrowing as it reaches the torch. This is again a structure of marvelous resiliency. It is extraordinarily so because of its precarious angle. (Its flexibility is best appreciated by standing on the torch balcony on a windy day—a dubious

privilege allowed only to Park Service maintenance personnel who reach it by ladder.)

During the ten years it took to construct Liberty in France, interest had never flagged. Her
right forearm and torch had been shipped in 1876
to America for its centennial, and in 1878 Liberty's
head was first viewed in Paris.

On October 24, 1881, the hundredth anniversary of the surrender of Yorktown, American Minister to France Levi P. Morton drove in the first
rivet of the outdoor phase of the assembly, and
by 1882 Liberty was rising steadily above the
houses surrounding it. Amidst a mass of scaffolding and the stares of curious onlookers, workmen
erected the skeletal ironwork of the interior and
then applied the copper clothing of the figure,
piece by piece. In the early 1880s, while the sculptor and the engineer were making their calcula-
tions to assure themselves that the colossal statue
was physically stable and would create the desired
visual effect as well, Parisians and visitors mar-
veled at the work of construction.

In the United States, the arm and torch had
been moved to New York's Madison Square,
where it remained on view from 1877 to 1884

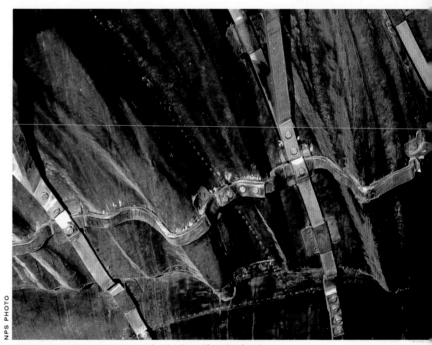

The statue's copper skin is itself relatively malleable. Rigid iron supports, approximating the shape of the copper, buttress the skin from the interior.

For a while, Liberty seemed like a surreal goddess, shrouded as she was in scaffolding and surrounded by the Lilliputian (comparatively speaking) neighborhood of narrow streets and low rooftops. The Paris workshop of "Gaget, Gauthier & Comp^{ie}," in which Liberty was given birth, appears to the left in this historic stereopticon photo. The statue was later disassembled and crated in preparation for the long journey to America.

(when it was shipped back to France to be connected to the rest of Liberty). New York's best hotel district surrounded the square, and parades often started or stopped there, making it altogether an ideal location for calling attention to the fund-raising effort. (A "Hotel Bartholdi" was for a time located near the square.)

The sheer size of Liberty was its greatest advertisement. "This stupendous specimen of womanhood," as described by an American reporter, had an "awful eye—some thirty inches from corner to corner" that "engulfed . . . [him] in her gaze." Curiosities of measurement were raptly described: "Her lips, from dimple to dimple, were as long as any walking stick."

By 1884, the completed Liberty stood in all her nobility and grace overlooking the rooftops of Paris. On June 11 the occasion was celebrated with a dinner at the American legation. On July 4 ceremonies marking the transference of the French gift were held, in which the statue was formally presented, complete with deed, by Ferdinand de Lesseps, of Suez Canal fame (Lesseps had become president of the Union Franco-Américaine upon Laboulaye's death the year before). The gift was accepted by American Minister Morton. Lib-

erty, however, would not fulfill her mission as ambassadress of friendship for two more years, during which time she awaited her departure for the United States and the completion of the huge pedestal she would grace at the gateway to the New World.

The Site and the Pedestal

On the other side of the Atlantic work was progressing, albeit slowly, on the pedestal. Its engineering was a critical factor in the stability of the statue and its design could seriously detract from or enhance Liberty's image, a consideration readily comprehended when it is realized that Liberty's pedestal and foundation are roughly equal to the statue itself in height.

The site on which Liberty was to be placed within New York Harbor had been carefully selected. Bartholdi's choice—Bedloe's Island—was a small, isolated island that would offer a view of Liberty unobstructed from every viewpoint, unlike the also-considered Governor's Island, a larger island that might compete in size with the statue. Both islands were federally owned, and in 1877 Congress put the decision upon the shoulders of General William T. Sherman, of Civil War fame. Sherman, bowing to the wishes of the sculptor, chose Bedloe's Island.

(Today we realize more than ever the sheer inspiration that lay behind the choosing of the site—and of the angle at which Liberty was ultimately placed in the harbor. She lies within the direct sight of passengers, aboardship, entering the harbor through the Narrows. Her image seems to change as the ship draws nearer, first appearing as if striding across the water in greeting and then stabilizing so that she never *quite* turns from her viewers. We must marvel at Bartholdi's genius in appreciating such considerations.)

It had also been decided that the pedestal was to be constructed in the center of the island's mid-nineteenth-century Fort Wood, whose outside walls formed an aesthetically pleasing eleven-pointed star. (The fort, constructed for the protection of the city, was no longer in active use.) Although the fort ultimately proved to be an excellent choice, it did present—with its "bomb-proof" masses of stone masonry—unanticipated difficulties in excavation that would slow progress considerably.

The colossal statue of course required a colossal pedestal (in actuality about the size of a ten-story building), one that would retain its essentially subordinate character. In other words, the pedestal had to be designed so that the statue remained the focus of attention. Site, pedestal, statue: All would have to be well integrated in order to form an architectural and aesthetic whole.

A number of designs for the pedestal were considered and rejected. The first design—a hexagonal structure with overtones of a medieval fortress, probably the work of Viollet-le-Duc—was widely reproduced. (This design appeared on the Philadelphia centennial medal of 1876 and, curiously, in modified form on the program for the 1886 dedication in New York, long after the design had been discarded.) A design of Bartholdi's was also for a time considered: A small, square pedestal atop a massive, stepped pyramid, it perhaps emphasized the influence ancient Egypt yet wielded upon him, although possibly the sculptor had in mind the thirteen-stepped pyramid which backs the great seal of the United States.

These designs were replaced by the work of Richard Morris Hunt, a well-known, Paris-educated architect of the day who in 1881 was chosen to design the pedestal. In the course of his work, Hunt corresponded with the sculptor regarding certain aspects of the project. He considered Bartholdi's pyramid and again rejected it, but the design Hunt proposed was likewise reminiscent

The unevenly textured granite and variety of forms used in Liberty's pedestal effectively reduce its massiveness as it tapers toward the statue's feet. The pedestal's most prominent feature is the loggia, or gallery, with its Doric columns. From the balcony, which overhangs the pedestal below, visitors to Liberty Island can enjoy the highest view of the harbor that is available outside the statue itself.

Throughout the day sunlight reflects on the gold surface of Liberty's torch.

committee decided the design was so great an improvement that it gave its approval anyway. It was a late date—the summer of 1884, when the statue was already completed and awaiting shipment, and the cornerstone had already been ceremoniously laid. But the design was worthy of the wait. Indeed, Hunt had accomplished a truly remarkable achievement—the blending of integrity of design and scale that would complement the statue itself in every way.

On July 20 the ferry *Bartholdi* chugged across the harbor to make its first trip in the shuttling of supplies to Bedloe's Island. A small railroad had been built there to facilitate the moving about of the stone.

The committee's efforts to keep costs down on the pedestal required the large-scale use of concrete—technically an artificial stone and a building material not yet in general use—instead of the more expensive granite. (It thus may have marked the turning point in the popularity of concrete in modern construction.) The concrete would be reinforced by the metal work that would anchor the pedestal to the statue.

The pedestal's foundation, at 11,680 cubic yards, was the largest single concrete mass built up to that time. The foundation mass is 52 feet 10 inches high, above a bottom foundation whose height is 13 feet above mean low water. It is 91 feet square at the bottom and 65 feet square at the top, and solid except for a 10-foot-square shaft in the center. The engineer-in-chief of the foundation, another Civil War veteran, General Charles P. Stone had assured the committee prior to construction that concrete would save unnecessary weight, and also be "much cheaper than the same amount of good stone masonry."

Concrete was again employed in the pedestal proper, the committee rejecting all initial bids for building the pedestal completely of granite as being too high. And it approved Stone's proposal that only the facing be of granite, with the backing of concrete. The statue was to be anchored to the pedestal by embedding four huge steel girders at right angles in the interior walls of the pedestal at the 29-foot level; 55 feet higher (5 feet below the top), additional girders were laid. Beams connecting the two sets of girders would continue up into the statue and become an integral part of the armature. The anchorage illustrates the principle of reinforced concrete: where the compressive strength of concrete combines with the tensile strength of steel so that, when subjected to bending forces, each material compensates for the other's weakness.

of an ancient Egyptian wonder—in this case, the *Pharos of Alexandria*, a lighthouse. This design appeared in the 1883 journal publishing the official engineering statistics for the statue proper, but was scrapped by Hunt as part of the committee's eleventh-hour move to reduce costs, in view of the less-than-successful efforts at fund-raising. (The *World* had not yet begun its campaign.) Aside from this consideration, the American Committee was concerned that the pedestal, at 114 feet (exclusive of its foundation), would overwhelm the statue. Hunt was directed to reduce the pedestal's height and redesign the upper part, leaving its lower segment, for which granite had already been quarried, untouched.

The architect's new design reduced the pedestal's height to 89 feet, but it ironically called for a more complex stonework that would increase the cost of the work by $20,000. Nevertheless, the

July 4, 1986

The pedestal and statue, considered separately, are thus examples of two opposing principles: Simplified, the pedestal relies upon mass for stability, the statue upon an iron skeleton. Whereas the walls of the pedestal, narrowing from 17 feet, 6 inches thick at the base to 6 feet thick at the top, bear their own weight, the copper pieces of the statue, 3/32 of an inch thick, transfer their weight to the interior armature.

The people of the period, unused to structures of such towering heights, feared that the statue might fall over if subjected to stress. It was to allay such fears that the public was confidently assured that to overturn the monument a windstorm would have to invert the whole island.

Reinforced concrete, skeleton construction, Bessemer steel, the passenger elevator, electric lighting—all were developments that occurred between the late 1860s and the mid-1880s, a period coinciding with the time from Liberty's conception to her completion. All along the way these innovative ideas were in one way or another incorporated into Liberty. (Provision was made for an elevator although the lack of funds prevented its installation for about twenty years.) And so the monument that began simply as a daring form for a lighthouse became in the course of construction a pacesetter in the application of modern technology, an astonishing example of the successful union of art and engineering.

"On April 22, 1886, the last stone of the pedestal was swung into place and the jubilant workmen showered into the mortar a collection of silver coins from their own pockets." America was ready to receive the great gift destined to become the best-known and most beloved statue in the world.

The French had not been idle. The statue had been ready for shipment since January of 1885, the pieces having been packed into 214 specially constructed wooden cases, each marked so that reassembly could be readily accomplished. Wood and metal together comprised a weight of 500,000 pounds, which was shipped by train from Paris to Rouen, where it was placed aboard the warship, the *Isère*. The French ship left with its distinguished passenger on May 21, 1885, and docked in New York Harbor a month later.

(It might be reasonably speculated that the familiar figure was missed in the city of her birth, for soon after her departure, a quarter-scale replica was constructed in Paris, paid for by New Yorkers living in Paris. It stands today on the Île des Cygnes, appropriately near the Eiffel Tower.)

Liberty, it is fair to say, would not have been possible for men less inspired than those into whose hands her fate was placed. Laboulaye, Bartholdi, Eiffel, Hunt, Stone, Pulitzer, Lesseps, Evarts—the list is an accumulation of minds each imprinted with its own particular stamp of brilliance. It is our great fortune that these men were there—at the right time and the right place—to perform their roles, large or small, in a drama that without each of them would have suffered or perhaps even failed. Just as remarkable is the almost certain fact that none of these men ever felt a twinge of doubt as to the ultimate success of what they were doing. Liberty herself carries on this tradition in the confidence with which she has greeted each day for nearly a hundred years.

The French tricolor flies from atop the uncompleted pedestal as Americans enthusiastically welcome the Isère *and her cargo, the crated Statue of Liberty.*

The steel and stone monoliths of New York's skyline symbolize the great age of technology of which Liberty's innovative engineering was an early part.

MUSEUM OF THE CITY OF NEW YORK

Center spread: Boats and people flock to the harbor to celebrate the statue's centennial. Photo by Jake Rajs/Image Bank.

Liberty Enlightening the World

In spite of the wet, foggy weather, everyone who could walk, ride, or ferry to Manhattan's lower shore was on hand to watch the unveiling of *Liberty Enlightening the World*. Even those who had previously ignored or criticized the project now joined in acclaiming Liberty's long-delayed debut on this day to remember, October 28, 1886.

A grand parade through the New York streets and a colorful flotilla of boats in the harbor preceded the numerous speeches by dignitaries, presided over by President Grover Cleveland. Over on the island, draped by the French tricolor—that nation's historic symbol of freedom, Liberty waited. But her sculptor was not so patient, and even before the last speech was finished, the excited Bartholdi—anticipating his cue—triggered the device rigged to unveil the face that would become the most famous in America.

That act was the signal to release all the feelings of excitement that throbbed in pent-up hearts that day—feelings that had to do with much more than the unveiling of a popular monument. Patriotism, liberty, justice, brotherhood—and the memory of all who had died for freedom: These were the things that were being celebrated on that memorable day. Foghorns bellowed their loud response, punctuated by the sharp reports of a twenty-one-gun salute from all the batteries in the harbor, ashore and afloat. (Fireworks had been planned, but because of the rain they were postponed for several days.) And Liberty's torch was illuminated with a flame that, though disappointingly tiny to those viewing it, would cast a powerful beam throughout the world.

President Cleveland had affirmed in his speech the political idea that linked Americans and Frenchmen so closely: the belief that a republican form of government was essential for liberty to exist. The gift, he said, demonstrated "the kinship of republics, and conveys to us the assurance that in our efforts to commend to mankind the excellence of a government resting upon popular will, we will have beyond the American continent a steadfast ally." But the president also spoke of a missionary statue, and his words were a vow for all Americans:

> We will not forget that Liberty has here made her home; nor shall her chosen altar be neglected. Willing votaries will constantly keep alive its fires, and these shall gleam upon the shores of our sister republic in the East. Reflected thence, and joined with answering rays, a stream of light shall pierce the darkness of ignorance and man's oppression, until liberty enlightens the world.

The Symbolism of Light

Liberty's light was an integral and critically important consideration in the development of the statue from the time of her conception. When the Union Franco-Américaine first proposed a statue dedicated to liberty, it announced that "at night a luminous aureole projected from the head will radiate on the far flowing waves of the ocean." The monument thus would be a functioning lighthouse as well as an artistic creation. And when Congress accepted the statue two years later, it authorized the president to maintain it as a "beacon" and as a "monument of art," placing it in the care of the Lighthouse Board.

Bartholdi designed the statue before the development of electric lighting. He imagined light radiating only from the diadem, with a lookout perhaps stationed on the observation platform around the torch. The flame, at that point, was to have no *useful* purpose.

Advances in lighting technology changed this plan. One month before the 1886 dedication, the decision was reached—the sculptor concurring—to light the torch electrically.

Edward Moran's 1886 painting depicts the unveiling of Liberty amidst an excited assemblage of people and boats in the harbor.

Edward Moran 1886

It was proposed that the light be placed outside the torch, on its platform, leaving the all-metal torch itself intact, the idea being that in this way the shaft of electric light reflected skyward would illumine the passing clouds and make the light visible to ships thirty, forty, or perhaps even a hundred miles out to sea.

Lieutenant John Millis, Corps of Engineers expert employed to install the lighting, rejected the idea on practical grounds. Placing a light on the outdoor platform, he said, would "dazzle" pilots navigating in the harbor nearby. Millis' solution was radical: to cut from the copper torch two rows of circular "windows," eleven and ten inches in diameter, to allow light from inside the torch to escape horizontally.

But the result was disappointing. Observers on shore at the dedication ceremony could hardly see the light from the island. Bartholdi complained that the little flame cast the light of a glowworm.

In 1892 an attempt was made to improve upon the lighting, altering the configuration of the torch even more. A belt of glass, eighteen inches in height, replaced one of the rows of circular windows. By then, also, a skylight of red, white,

and yellow glass allowed light to escape vertically, and in the diadem a short-lived experiment involved the installation of red, white, and blue lamps. The Lighthouse Board confidently announced its decision:

NOTICE TO MARINERS.
(No. 90, of 1892.)

⸺⟡⸺

UNITED STATES OF AMERICA—NEW YORK.

⸺⟡⸺

LIBERTY ENLIGHTENING THE WORLD.

Notice is hereby given that, on or about October 21, 1892, the following changes will be made in the lights and illumination of the Statue of Liberty Enlightening the World, inside Fort Wood, Bedloes Island, New York Bay, New York.

In addition to the light now shown from the torch there will be a vertical beam of red and yellow light seen only by reflection from the haze or dust in the air.

The face and bust of the statue will be illuminated by a powerful search light from one of the salients of the fort.

The coronet will be decorated with red, white, and blue incandescent electric lights.

The pedestal will continue to be illuminated as heretofore by arc lamps within the salients and not visible outside the fort.

BY ORDER OF THE LIGHT-HOUSE BOARD:

JAMES A. GREER,
Rear-Admiral, U. S. Navy,
Chairman.

OFFICE OF THE LIGHT-HOUSE BOARD:
Washington, D. C., September 30, 1892.

Still the statue did not emit enough light for it to function effectively as a lighthouse. The absence of technological know-how was frustrating and seemingly unsolvable, a fact officially recognized in 1902 when the statue was transferred from the administration of the Lighthouse Board to the War Department. But although the lighting would now serve no practical purpose, its symbolic ramifications attained greater and greater importance, as demonstrated during World War I.

In 1916, the New York *World*, in shades of its 1885 pedestal fund-raising campaign, called upon the people once again—this time for funds to improve Liberty's night-time appearance. War darkened Europe, but the United States remained a bastion of liberty and peace. Once again the public responded, with $30,000 for the floodlighting of the statue at night and the redesigning of the torch in glass. It was at this time in her history that Liberty assumed the night-time glow by which she is so often remembered.

Rudimentary night-lighting previously had failed to counteract the effects of oxidation. As the copper darkened with age, a green patina slowly developed, and the statue reflected increasingly less light than did its lighter-colored granite base. Bartholdi had in 1887 bemoaned this situation,

but his half-in-jest solution—to gild the statue—and that of Millis'—to paint it white (offered primarily as a means of making it visible to ships)—were economically or aesthetically unsound. The 1916 floodlighting system represented the application of a new technology to a problem that had plagued the monument from almost its inception. Now, installed at the base of the statue and at other low-level locations on Bedloe's Island, 246 projectors producing 1,200,000 lumens bathed the statue in, at last, a satisfying glow.

The torch, too, was greatly improved. Gutzon Borglum (later to attain national prominence as the sculptor of Mount Rushmore, a similarly daring project), supervised the resculpting of the torch, in which copper was removed in about six-hundred pieces and replaced by an equal number of pieces of amber-colored cathedral glass. The copper that Borglum did not remove formed crisscrossing strips about an inch in width that supported the glass. To further the enhancement of the lighted torch, Borglum placed more of the lightly colored glass at the flame's tip than he did at its base. The resulting translucent torch emitted a constant light of about 250,000 lumens (equivalent to 13,250 watts in incandescent lamps) and

THE NEW-YORK HISTORICAL SOCIETY; PHOTO BY MAJOR HAMILTON MAXWELL

an additional 95,000 lumens in lamps placed upon a series of flashers which imitated the flicker of a natural flame.

President Woodrow Wilson inaugurated the new lighting in a spectacular ceremony, which he and French Ambassador Jules Jusserand watched from aboard the presidential yacht standing at anchor in the harbor. Ships bedecked with lights surrounded the statue. As the lights went on, aviatrix Ruth Law circled the statue, trailing behind her plane the word *Liberty* in bold letters in the night-time sky.

But all was not perfect. The new floodlighting system, innovative though it was, created unseemly shadows on Liberty's face, and from some angles it had the odd effect of separating Liberty from her pedestal. Finally, corrosion affected the system's outdoor components.

A second floodlighting system, installed in 1931, remedied these defects and produced approximately two million lumens, nearly doubling the light produced by the 1916 system. Jose Laval, the French premier's daughter, turned on the lights that would initiate the new system. From the topmost (102nd) floor of the newly built Empire State Building, she transmitted a radio signal to an airplane flying above the statue. A responding signal from the plane triggered an electric eye that turned on the lights that would transform Liberty once again.

With World War II, the history of light as a symbol of liberty and enlightenment acquired a new chapter. The war had caused the "lights of freedom" to go out all over Europe, and—except for an aircraft warning light—it brought darkness to the Statue of Liberty. America's symbol defended against enemy assault with a real blackout, broken only to mark D-Day, the beginning of the liberation of France and eventually Europe. As a result, the new lighting of 1946 created considerable public interest.

The year 1976 saw the installation of a still more powerful lighting system, timed to the celebration of the nation's bicentennial. With this last improvement, Liberty truly became the radiant night-time beacon envisioned by Bartholdi nearly a century before.

Liberty: A Uniquely American Symbol

Gradually *Liberty Enlightening the World* became known more simply as *The Statue of Liberty*. Her emergence as a national symbol took place primarily during World War I, when she replaced *Columbia*, a female figure that had been a popular representation of America since the Revolution. Liberty was now a celebrity. Her picture appeared everywhere: In posters printed in the millions Liberty appealed to Americans to buy bonds to finance the war, and with amazing success. In the four Liberty loan drives of 1917–1918, the U.S. Government sold about $15 billion in bonds, equal to about half the total cost of the war. The more imaginative posters enlivened Liberty with poses and speeches, occasionally taking the statue from its pedestal and making it the female counterpart of Uncle Sam. In several posters, Liberty appeared draped in the American flag; in others she was represented as a warrior.

The provocative use of Liberty's image ended with World War I, but the statue's contemporary relevance was evidenced again as Europe edged toward a new war in the 1930s. The totalitarian crisis of that decade coincided with the celebration of Liberty's fiftieth anniversary.

MICHAEL SKOTT/IMAGE BANK

The effectiveness of Liberty's present lighting system is dramatically demonstrated. The smoke is from fireworks commemorating the nation's bicentennial.

After the restoration the crowds returned. Even from the back she is a magnificent symbol.

HARPER'S WEEKLY

A JOURNAL OF CIVILIZATION

Vol. LIII   New York, October 9, 1909   No. 2755

JAY MAISEL

A NEW KIND OF GULL IN NEW YORK HARBOR

Wilbur Wright, who was under contract to give demonstrations with his aeroplane during the Hudson-Fulton celebration, made a most spectacular flight on September 29th, when he circled the Statue of Liberty in New York Harbor, and returned to the starting-point on Governors Island without mishap, reaching a speed of fifty miles an hour

Liberty's stoic features were a reassurance to millions of Americans during the dark days of World War II.

In planning for the event, the National Park Service (which had taken over the administration of the monument from the War Department in 1933) did not confine the celebration to either Liberty's site or her anniversary date. The full year of 1936 was given over to the commemoration, and the Park Service disseminated information and suggested the kinds of activities that would be appropriate for the observance. People all over the nation joined in the observance of the Liberty they revered deeply, although many had never even seen her.

Poetry, essay, and radio-script contests were the more ambitious projects. More than a hundred thousand high-school students submitted entries in an essay competition on "What the Statue of Liberty Means to the American People," sponsored by the Ladies Auxiliary to the Veterans of Foreign Wars. A poetry contest was sponsored by the National Life Conservation Society, with the

cooperation of the Park Service, and the sixty best poems were published. The winning entry, by Sheila Jane Crooke of Urbana, Illinois, painted a vivid picture of the persecution of the Jews in Germany and the war in Spain. It concluded with this reminder to Americans of the threat of war in Europe and a paean to Liberty:

In London I talked to a woman
who'd just received a government gas-mask.
"Do you think," I said, "that you'll ever use that?"
She shook her head.
"I don't know," she answered.
"I don't know—but—I'm afraid."

I'm afraid, they said, I'm afraid, I'm afraid.
All over Europe they said: I'm afraid, I'm afraid.

When we steamed into New York Harbor the other day
I got up very early,
So as to be sure of getting a good, long look
at Liberty, standing there.

So proud, so peacefully reassuring, so—
God bless you, old girl! So unafraid!

A New Meaning: Brotherhood

By the 1930s the ethnic character of the American people had changed radically from what it had been when the statue was erected fifty years before. The time between Liberty's dedication and rededication witnessed the "new" immigration—the arrival in America of millions of people from southern and eastern Europe and from the Near East. This mass migration and the recurrent threats to personal liberty since World War I had firmly established Liberty, herself an immigrant, as the beloved welcomer to a friendly home. Liberty had grown far beyond a commemoration of an international friendship; she had become the symbol of America as a nation and then as a refuge for the oppressed. For the immigrants who once crowded the decks of incoming ships for a glimpse of her, Liberty offered in her outstretched torch the promise of freedom and a better life.

Edward Corsi, one-time commissioner of the immigrant processing center at Ellis Island, recalls the "wonder, excitement, and apprehension of a ten-year-old Italian boy's first contact with America."

Guiseppe and I held tightly to stepfather's hands, while Liberta and Helvetia clung to mother. Passengers all about us were crowding against the rail. Jabbered conversation, sharp cries, laughs and cheers—a steadily rising din filled the air. Mothers and fathers lifted up the babies so that they too could see, off to the left, the Statue of Liberty.

I looked at that statue with a sense of bewilderment, half doubting its reality. Looming shadowy through the mist, it brought silence to the decks. . . . This symbol of America—this enormous expression of what we had all been taught was the inner meaning of this new country we were coming to—inspired awe in the hopeful immigrants. Many older persons among us, burdened with a thousand memories of what they were leaving behind, had been openly weeping ever since we entered the narrower waters on our final approach toward the unknown. Now somehow steadied, I suppose, by the concreteness of the symbol of America's freedom, they dried their tears.

Even as early as 1883, Liberty had inspired feelings such as these. "The New Colossus," the poem that has come to speak for the "new" Liberty ("Mother of Exiles") and that now appears on a bronze plaque permanently displayed at the monument, was written in that year by Emma Lazarus. When approached to write a poem in behalf of the pedestal-fund campaign, this genteel lady of New York society, whose reputation as a poet was well established, was at first reluctant to "produce to order." But soon, affected by Liberty's spirit and stirred deeply by the massacres then taking place in Russia—oppression that would lead to the mass exodus of Jews from that country—she agreed. In writing it, the poet, herself a Sephardic Jew, gave expression to the universal protest against the pogroms and codified restrictions limiting Jewish worship and economic activity that followed Tsar Alexander II's assassination in 1881. Her impassioned words are engraved on the memories of millions of Americans:

Not like the brazen giant of Greek fame,
With conquering limbs astride from land to land;
Here at our sea-washed, sunset gates shall stand
A mighty woman with a torch, whose flame
Is the imprisoned lightning, and her name
Mother of Exiles. From her beacon-hand
Glows world-wide welcome; her mild eyes command
The air-bridged harbor that twin cities frame.
"Keep, ancient lands, your storied pomp!" cries she
With silent lips. "Give me your tired, your poor,
Your huddled masses yearning to breathe free,
The wretched refuse of your teeming shore.
Send these, the homeless, tempest-tost to me,
I lift my lamp beside the golden door!"

For the millions of immigrants who have come to America from all over the world, Liberty elicits some powerful and very personal emotions.

The Statue of Liberty Today

The Statue of Liberty dates its modern history from 1933, when the National Park Service took over its administration. Previously, it had been part of the War Department's Fort Wood army base on Bedloe's Island (even after it had been declared a national monument on October 15, 1924). And previous to that, from 1886 to 1902, Liberty was administered by the Lighthouse Board, in accordance with Congress' 1877 resolution to operate the statue as a lighthouse. Throughout this period, the military installation occupied the larger portion of Bedloe's Island and Liberty the smaller. Since 1933, the National Park Service has gradually changed the monument into a park and has landscaped it to interpret the American ideals of liberty and pluralism.

In 1933, the Army still retained control over most of the island. The Park Service looked dimly upon this arrangement, since its long-range plans depended upon the removal of the army base al-

together. On-site inspections disclosed that the Army had placed visitor facilities poorly. The island's clutter of warehouses, barracks, and miscellaneous structures detracted from the dignity and beauty of the statue. The public, after debarking, had to pass by a warehouse located on a dilapidated, hundred-year-old dock, and adding to the inappropriateness of Liberty's setting were a prominently placed "comfort station," a metallic frankfurter stand, and sixteen unsightly buildings.

It was generally agreed that Liberty deserved better. Before the close of 1933, less than a year after the National Park Service had assumed responsibility for the statue, the Secretary of the Interior requested of the Secretary of War that all of Bedloe's Island be made part of the monument in order to provide a proper setting for Liberty.

The secretary's request foreshadowed a series of changes and expansions that have continued down to the present. In 1937, the army relin-

STEPHEN GREEN-ARMYTAGE/IMAGE BANK

Two familiar sights in New York Harbor: Liberty, bastion of freedom, is passed by the Staten Island ferry, carrying passengers between Staten Island and Manhattan. Regular commuters take the statue in stride.

Liberty, whose colossal 302-foot height once dominated the New York skyline, is now dwarfed by many structures, including the huge twin towers of the World Trade Center, completed in 1973. The 110-story towers, each 1,353 feet high, are New York's tallest buildings.

This spectacular nighttime panorama extends from the World Trade Center and the Statue of Liberty to the illuminated buildings of lower Manhattan.

quished control of its part of the island to the Park Service. It was followed in 1939 by a master plan that called for all of the existing structures, except for Fort Wood itself, to be torn down and, where necessary, replaced. When World War II compelled a realignment of the nation's priorities, the pace of redevelopment, by then well underway, slowed, and it was not until after the war, in the early 1950s, that the last of the army buildings finally came down.

On October 3, 1956, Bedloe's Island—originally named for the Dutchman who was granted the island when New York (New Amsterdam) was under Dutch sovereignty—was renamed "Liberty Island," and today the whole of the island is used as the setting for America's most famous monument. Ferries cross in front of the statue, offering

visitors a view from nearly every side, and the area set aside for special events has an unobstructed view of New York's famous skyline. The new entrance, built at the end of a long, hedge-lined mall, fulfills the master-plan requirement of "ample simplicity," providing a fitting approach to Liberty. The park has become, as well, a welcome refuge for many who wish only to escape for a time the bustle of metropolitan New York.

Within the statue's pedestal an elevator carries visitors beyond the floors that house park exhibits and administrative offices to an outdoor observation balcony at the top of the pedestal. A stairway spirals all the way to the head and down again, 168 steps each way, complete with two rest platforms. The interior had always been meant to

be viewed; the stairways had been part of the original design. It is a strange sensation to ascend the stairway. One feels rather like a traveler in a Jules Verne or Isaac Asimov novel, and it is difficult to remember that the enclosure is not the massive shell it appears to be but only a fragile copper skin.

The eerie feeling is dispersed, however, on reaching the observation platform within Liberty's head. On a clear day, a breathtaking panorama of the New York Harbor can be seen from twenty-five windows, "jewels" of the seven-rayed diadem. The tablet in Liberty's left hand, bearing the date of America's independence in Roman numerals, can best be seen from here. Liberty's torch, closed to the public, can be reached only by means of a ladder. Park maintenance personnel use this access to maintain the lighting equipment of the torch.

It is hard to realize, when viewing the impressive skyline of modern Manhattan, that Liberty's size once dominated the entire scene here. For thirteen years she remained the tallest structure in existence, towering over such structures as the Western Union Telegraph Building (1873) at 230 feet, Trinity Church (1846) at 286 feet, the Tribune Building, and the Brooklyn Bridge towers, 23 feet lower than the statue. It was not until 1899 that she began to be eclipsed in size, with the construction of St. Paul's Building—at 310 feet then the world's tallest building. In reviewing these facts, it finally comes home to us what a colossal undertaking the Statue of Liberty really was.

David Sarnoff (1891–1971), radio and television pioneer, from Russia, 1900

Albert Einstein (1879–1955),
eminent physicist, from Germany, 1933

The American Museum of Immigration

In 1955 the Secretary of the Interior entered into a cooperative agreement with the American Museum of Immigration, Inc., a private organization, to establish the American Museum of Immigration in the base of the statue. This was a way of formally recognizing that America was inherently a nation of immigrants. The agreement recognized the outstanding contributions that had

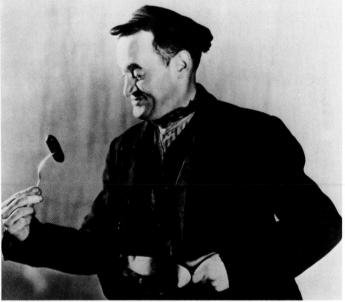

Barry Fitzgerald (1888–1961), award-winning actor, from Ireland, 1936

Samuel Gompers (1850–1924),
labor leader, from England, 1863

been made by "all liberty-seeking immigrants from throughout the entire world [to] a strong and free United States."

To provide room, the historic pedestal was altered by the addition of a two-tiered structure at the base, which served to house exhibits and other museum facilities. Actual construction began in 1962, and the museum was opened ten years later. Throughout this period of construction, the American Museum of Immigration, Inc., raised funds from more than seventy private organizations and from many individuals. About forty nationalities and ethnic groups are represented in the exhibits in some way, exhibits that dramatically demonstrate that America is indeed a nation of immigrants.

Above Liberty appears Ellis Island. Millions entered America through this immigration depot. Its Neo-Renaissance domes and arches are reminders of an era whose pathos has touched us all. The island is being revitalized and will soon be opened as still another chapter of America's historic past.

ELLIS ISLAND

Ellis Island, which lies just beyond the statue in New York Harbor, once represented for most New York-bound aliens their first experience in America. From 1892 until 1954, more than twelve million people—between half and three-quarters of all immigrants entering the United States during that period—passed through Ellis Island, all desperately eager to believe in the promise of the new land. New arrivals were examined briefly by doctors checking for obvious ailments—tuberculosis, lameness, trachoma (a parasitic eye disease), heart and respiratory difficulties. Inspectors cross-checked answers given aboard ship and recorded on manifest sheets. On its peak day, April 17, 1907, over 11,000 people were channeled through the maze-like system.

At first immigration was minimally restricted. The law forbade the acceptance of aliens likely to become public charges, but quixotically also forbade the contracting of work by immigrants prior to leaving their homelands. It also specifically excluded polygamists, anarchists, and imbeciles. Women traveling alone were "protected"—and their entries often delayed—lest they be gulled into working as prostitutes. After 1917 a literacy test in English or the immigrant's native language was an added requirement.

Despite such restrictions, few were actually excluded. Passports and visas were required, and inspectors questioned most people for only five to ten minutes. More than ninety-eight percent of all aliens seeking entry to America through Ellis Island were admitted. Dormitory, eating, and hospital facilities were developed for the few who were turned back and for those detained for further questioning or for medical treatment. A money exchange, post office, and railroad ticket office provided aid to the new Americans.

Restrictive immigration laws and new inspection procedures that had to be followed *prior* to emigrating were instituted in the 1920s. The Immigration Service, no longer having to process great numbers of entrants, continued its use of Ellis Island as an immigration station, but increasingly used the complex primarily as a detention and deportation center. The U.S. Public Health Service assumed responsibility for the operation of the Ellis Island hospital; during the world wars the military occupied considerable space there. When the Immigration Service abandoned Ellis Island in 1954, the station had for some time outlived its original purpose and its later functions.

For a time, the federal government attempted to dispose of Ellis Island to private bidders. But as the historic importance of the island became more evident, the unsuitability of its use for most private purposes was realized. In 1965 the island was added to the Statue of Liberty National Monument in recognition of the role the former immigration station had played as the gateway to the nation. This event also had the effect of reinforcing Liberty's identification with immigration.

In the meantime, the harsh weather of New York Harbor and the absence of any basic maintenance program caused the buildings to deteriorate rapidly, evidenced by rotting wood and fallen plaster. Many of the buildings suffered structural damage. The cost of restoration—tens of millions of dollars—seemed prohibitive. Besides, no agreement could be reached as to what parts should be preserved and/or restored. An ambitious proposal in 1966 by famed architect Philip Johnson to demolish most of the island's structures and erect a wall bearing the names of Ellis Island immigrants went unfunded. And the ferryboat *Ellis Island*, which from 1904 to 1954 plied between city and station, sank in 1968, leaving only the superstruc-

ture intact. In the 1970s the boat became a much photographed hulk, unsalvageable and symbolic of Ellis Island's fallen state.

The turnabout for Ellis Island—the commitment to save the island's historic structures—came when the nation celebrated its bicentennial. Starting in 1976, National Park Service guides took visitors on tours that simulated the immigrants' route: stops were made in the baggage room, the registration area (the Main Hall), a cafeteria, a social-service office area, and an area for querying detainees. And between 1978 and 1982 Congress appropriated $8,000,000 towards the island's development.

Although the National Park Service, even with this large sum, could not repair Ellis Island's facilities sufficiently to prevent them from deteriorating further, the future of the island as a historic site is now assured. The Statue of Liberty–Ellis Island Centennial Commission, formed in 1982, has as one of its goals the restoration and development of the Ellis Island immigration station in time for its centennial in 1992. The work, now privately funded, will cost more than $150,000,000.

THE TEST OF TIME

The embodiment of such an abstract idea as *liberty* in a physical monument presents a certain paradox. The structure deteriorates with time even though the idea it represents is universal and timeless. This is no less true of the Statue of Liberty than it was of the colossi of Egypt. Vigilance is necessary to preserve the symbol itself, as well as the idea.

Liberty, a product of a new technological era, has survived its first century, but the elements of deterioration have not gone unnoticed. The statue, originally reddish-brown in color, is now a pale green, the pure copper in which it was clad having oxidized to produce a patina, or *verdigris*. Unlike rust, which is the oxidized form of iron, verdigris after it has formed on copper ordinarily protects it from further corrosion.

The quite predictable formation of verdigris upon Liberty's exterior appears to have surprised a great many people, including its sculptor. For several decades, because the patina formed slowly and unevenly (in 1903 it was described as a "lichen-

On the evening of July 4, 1986, the Statue of Liberty became the centerpiece in a dazzling fireworks display in celebration of her centennial. Hundreds of thousands of people watched the once-in-a-lifetime spectacle from the nearby shores of New York and New Jersey.

NPS PHOTO

Visitors are rewarded for the long climb (168 steps) to Liberty's head by a unique view of the harbor from inside the crown.

Ferries such as the "Miss Liberty" carry visitors to and from the statue nearly every day of the year.

K. C. DENDOOVEN

These photos give a bird's-eye view of Liberty from several angles. Especially noticeable from this lofty approach are the ornamentation in the torch and the detail of the drapery about the right arm.

like covering"), the cleaning of the statue was seriously contemplated. The American Committee, which oversaw the daily operation of the statue at that time, took no action because of the cost and its own inadequate funds, and assumed the position that the verdigris was not damaging the metal anyway.

Exposure to the environment of New York Harbor finally forced the federal government to undertake major repairs. Early in the 1930s the armature of the torch arm was strengthened. (It was closed to the public in 1916 due to the difficulty of access to the torch—not, as some have speculated, because the arm developed a weakness.) Later in the decade, after a detailed inspection had been made, the National Park Service closed the statue to the public for a year and a half in order to remedy a number of problems that threatened the statue's very integrity.

The copper was in good condition, but much of the metal work in the supporting system had become badly corroded. Affected especially were the spiral stairs leading to the crown, the stairway in the pedestal, the ladder to the torch, and the iron supporting the spikes of the crown. Condensation had adversely affected the concrete. Nearly 70,000 rivets needed replacement. Rainwater seeping through the seams of the torch continually wet the spiral stairs at the top of the statue, drenching visitors. It also dripped down the elevator shaft in the pedestal and into the elevator.

Virtually all the needed repairs of the 1930s were accomplished with admirable speed as projects of the Works Progress Administration (WPA). In 1949 the addition of a heating system in the base of the statue further reduced problems of condensation as well as contributing to the comfort of the interior for its occupants.

The statue has now been repaired from top to bottom. Corrosion, made worse by acid rain, had weakened the iron supporting structure of the crown, the torch, and the torch arm as well as the spiral stairway to the head.

K. C. DENDOOVEN

Making Liberty "new" got under way in earnest in May 1982 when President Ronald Reagan announced the formation of the Statue of Liberty–Ellis Island Centennial Commission. He charged the commission with making recommendations for restoring the statue in time to celebrate, in 1986, the hundredth anniversary of its dedication. The commission's recommendations were carried out by a nonprofit foundation.

To complete the project a 300-ton aluminum scaffolding rising 250 feet was built to totally surround the statue. The American and French craftsmen employed on the project built a new torch with a gilded copper flame (the old torch of glass and copper is now on exhibit in the lobby) and they also replaced piece by piece each of the more than 1,700 interior iron supports with steel ones. This work and the cost of other improvements exceeded $80,000,000.

Liberty has again undergone renewal. The deterioration that has occurred in the relatively short span of 100 years is a lesson that illustrates how physically impermanent a symbol can be. The message of freedom and equality remains a strong and a vital one, but its expression through the Statue of Liberty will be valid only as long as that symbol emanates physically as well as symbolically an image of strength and well-being. Liberty deserves to be cared for in proportion to the love and affection the world holds for her—and that calls for a great deal of care indeed.

SUGGESTED READING

BARTHOLDI, FRÉDÉRIC AUGUSTE. *The Statue of Liberty Enlightening the World Described by the Sculptor.* New York: North American Review, 1885.

BLUMBERG, BARBARA. *Celebrating the Immigrant: An Administrative History of the Statue of Liberty National Monument 1952–1982.* U.S. Dept. of the Interior, National Park Service, Cultural Resource Management Study, No. 10. Boston: National Park Service, 1985.

BROWNSTONE, DAVID M., IRENE M. FRANCK, and DOUGLASS L. BROWNSTONE. *Island of Hope, Island of Tears.* New York: Rawson, Wade Publishers, Inc., 1979.

HANDLIN, OSCAR, AND THE EDITORS OF THE BOOK DIVISION, *Newsweek. Statue of Liberty.* New York: Newsweek, 1971.

NOVOTNY, ANN. *Strangers at the Door: Ellis Island, Castle Garden, and the Great Migration to America.* [1971] Old Greenwich, Ct.: The Chatham Press, Inc., 1984.

PITKIN, THOMAS M. *Keepers of the Gate: A History of Ellis Island.* New York: New York Univ. Press, 1975.

TRACHTENBERG, MARVIN. *The Statue of Liberty.* New York: Penguin Books, 1977.

Liberty: Heritage of the People

Perhaps the best way to comprehend the full impact of what the Statue of Liberty means to most people is to take the ferryboat that each year transports millions of people to and from Liberty Island. Awe, fascination, exhilaration—they are all there in the wonderfully individual faces of the people who leave their seats and rush to the rails to get the benefit of every possible moment in which *she* graces their sight. Excitement is conveyed through the air in a multiplicity of languages, and for the moment the inevitable hot dogs and Coke go untasted. It is as if a single, rapt purpose has overtaken us all.

Indeed, the Statue of Liberty is a sight that evokes a virtual torrent of emotions in the hearts of most Americans—and of many visitors to America as well. But in experiencing this sight it seems that there is one feeling that transcends all others. And that is, simply, affection. Strange that such a huge monument that is, after all, only copper, concrete, and iron should inspire such warmth.

But for all of us the Statue of Liberty has taken on such a symbolic meaning that it is virtually impossible to view her in a coldly objective light. We scoff at old arguments about her place in the world of art; such considerations are insignificant and petty. After all is said and done, even her origins have little bearing on the way we feel about her. They, and her colossal measurements, are merely a matter of curiosity.

It is her *presence* that is everything. Her arms are *our* arms, her eyes *our* eyes. Her torch radiates our own promise, and her massive form confirms our strength.

She is a kind of goddess, and we revere her, but she is eminently approachable. We are her intimates. She is a phenomenon, not of nature but of the remarkable ability of man himself, when inspired, to inspire others.

So, Miss Liberty, lift up your lamp—forever if you can—and may America never cease to be the "golden door" of freedom and opportunity.

A hundred years after her establishment, the Lady is viewed from land, sea and air.

K. C. DENDOOVEN

Books in this series: Acadia, Alcatraz Island, Arches, Blue Ridge Parkway, Bryce Canyon, Canyon de Chelly, Cape Cod, Capitol Reef, Channel Islands, Civil War Parks, Crater Lake, Death Valley, Denali, Dinosaur, Everglades, Fort Clatsop, Gettysburg, Glacier, Glen Canyon–Lake Powell, Grand Canyon, Grand Teton, Great Smoky Mountains, Haleakala, Hawaii Volcanoes, Lake Mead–Hoover Dam, Lassen Volcanic, Lincoln Parks, Mount Rainier, Mount Rushmore, Mount St. Helens, National Park Service, National Seashores, North Cascades, Olympic, Petrified Forest, Redwood, Rocky Mountain, Scotty's Castle, Sequoia–Kings Canyon, Shenandoah, Statue of Liberty, Theodore Roosevelt, Virgin Islands, Yellowstone, Yosemite, Zion.

Published by KC Publications · Box 14883 · Las Vegas, NV 89114

The face of Lady Liberty.
Photo by Dan Cornish/ESTO

Back Cover: Liberty's most telling symbol — her colossal torch of truth.
Photo by Robert Kristofik/Image Bank

Printed by Dong-A Printing Co., Ltd., Seoul, Korea
Separations by Kwangyangsa Co., Ltd.
Typography by Stanley Stillion